# Deciding How to Publish Your Book

John Avery

DECIDING HOW TO PUBLISH YOUR BOOK
Copyright © John Avery, 2017

Formatting and cover design by D.J. Natelson. Cover image by Wikimedia user Σ64.

# CONTENTS

# ABOUT THE AUTHOR

John Avery is the author of *The Name Quest – explore the names of God to grow in faith and get to know Him better* (Morgan James Publishing, 2015). The Name Quest has been reviewed in Midwest Book Reviews and Christian News Northwest among others. It won the Oregon Christian Writers' Cascade Award for nonfiction.

John is a trained teacher with over thirty years experience as a Bible teaching pastor, small group leader, and missionary. He has lived in England, Israel, Africa, and the Caribbean, ministering with Youth With A Mission (YWAM) and local churches. He and his wife, Janet, now make their home in Oregon. John likes to hike, snowshoe, and cross country ski. John writes a Bible devotional at www.BibleMaturity.com one of which won the Oregon Christian Writers' Cascade Award for published devotionals. He maintains a comprehensive resource for all the names of God at www.NamesForGod.net.

"John Avery's advice is sound and informative. *Deciding How to Publish Your Book* is recommended for writers who hope to publish a book."

—Nick Harrison, WordServe Literary Agency.


"Make no mistake: John Avery isn't lucky. He worked long and hard and it paid off big-time. His first book won the 2016 *Oregon Christian Writers'* Cascade Award for Best Non-fiction Book. That's why I'm so glad John has kept on writing. Read this booklet once to see what he says. Then read it again to hear what he means. If you do, you'll learn how to ask smart publishing questions—and discern the right answers. Here is to *your* success!"

—David Sanford, Author, Editor, and Literary Agent with www.credocommunications.net.


"In this small booklet, John Avery has laid out the three possible paths to publication and leads potential authors in the direction that best fits their particular publishing goals. Success in the publishing field often depends on making the right choices. This must-have resource helps both new and experienced writers make the choices that will lead to success."

—Sally E. Stuart, Founder, *Christian Writers' Market Guide.*

"Whether you are pursuing a traditional large-house publishing contract or considering publishing on your own, this resource is a must-read. Cutting through the confusion, John Avery points out the pros and cons of each publishing option available to us in today's exciting times. Well-balanced and insightful."

—Christina Tarabochia, Traditionally published award-winning author, DIY-published award-winning author, & Publisher at Ashberry Lane, an award-winning Indie press.

# Deciding How to Publish Your Book

# INTRODUCTION

When I wrote my first book, *The Name Quest*, I planned to self-publish it—literally. I intended to set up my own publishing company and assemble a team with the right skills and experience to accomplish the task. I did not want to hack my way into the confusing jungle of publishers and contracts and endure the soul destroying process of proposals followed by long waits for rejections. Part of my research was to compare the packages offered by a few large "self-publishing" companies and answer the two most important questions: What exactly does a publisher need to do to produce a book and make it succeed in the marketplace? How much can an author really accomplish when it comes to getting a book into bookstores?

I read a lot. I asked a lot of questions. Then, just before I took the leap, Morgan James Publishing offered me a contract to publish *The Name Quest*. Their offer was better than what I could accomplish on my own, so I signed. But on my three-year journey I learned many lessons that I want to pass on to you.

My research included several publishers and other companies within the industry. It does not matter which companies they are because they offered similar menus of services and the publishers made similar claims about their ability to market my book. Giving a critique of any particular publisher is not my goal with this book; there are enough websites that warn authors of rogue publishers, and besides, I don't want to risk being sued.

Neither do I want you to sue me! So what I offer here is a set of questions that you, as an author on the journey to publication of a book, will do well to ask as you decide which route you want to take. The bottom line is that you are responsible for your book—not me, not your editor, not even your publisher.

## Who This Book Is For

If you are an aspiring author of a printed book, or your experience of book publishing has left you confused or dissatisfied, this book is for you. My experience has been in Christian non-fiction written for a broad market. However, the principles that I address apply to fiction and to non-religious books. I will define three broad publishing models and the pros and cons of each model. Then I will suggest ways to determine which model best suits your publishing goals. And by "publishing" I include book sales; a publisher that simply produces a book but is unable to present it to the right market is doing an author no favors.

Some specialty publishers don't fit my three broad models so well. I'm a lousy poet (and now you know it). If you have a book that is written for a niche market (family memoir, local interest, academia, organization, or hobby group), a children's book, a work in a foreign language, a coffee table book, or if you only want an e-book format, then you will get less from this book. I recommend you approach publishers that have a proven track record in producing and selling such books. In the case of e-books, there are plenty of resources available to help you, and distribution is easy.

## Core Values

Some people feel awkward about wanting to make money or to gather fans. Perhaps the world would be a better place if every creative gift was offered at cost and no one paid attention to followings. But that's not our world and there is nothing wrong with money or fans. If you have a valuable product or service then legitimate measures of its value are the amount people will pay for it and the number of people who take interest in it. Most of us want to maximize the number of lives we can influence. The number of people liking our book is a reasonable indication of whether we are accomplishing our goals. Even if commerce and fame have little or no place in your plan, don't feel guilty making a profit; it is another sign of goal achievement and shows that your book is priced right for the market.

We all have different reasons for writing our books and it is essential to understand our own values and goals before we choose our publishing route. Your goals and values will be challenged.

There are some people for whom profit or popularity is the primary driving force. If you are among them, I recommend that you find out what sells best and select models and methods that maximize market exposure and your income.

My own goals came from a mixture of spiritual and literary values. *The Name Quest* encapsulates deep biblical principles about relationship with God. I wanted to help people grow closer to Him, become more like Him, and deepen in faith through a study on the names of God. In addition, I aimed for a well-written, readable, and biblically accurate book. I have no desire to churn out numerous productions written in a week or so to feed the latest fad and a fat bank account.

My guess is that your values and goals are not so different from mine. You have a story that will entertain, knowledge that will feed inquisitive minds, an experience that others can benefit from, lessons to teach, revelations to impart, or answers to common questions. You want to help people, and the more people you can help, the better.

Exercise: What part does this book play in your life? In your writing career or ministry? (Sole book vs one of many. The book acts like a brochure to promote other products or services.)

What are your non-negotiable core values when it comes to writing and publishing? Be aware of a publisher's genres, including the ones published under other imprints (which are like sub-publishers under the main publishing house). Sometimes, morally questionable material is published under a separate imprint.

How much do factual accuracy and excellence matter to you? (This will determine, for instance, how thorough your research needs to be, how important editing is, and the quality and style of designers and printers.)

What will "success" look like for your book? (Perhaps maximizing the number of lives touched by the message, product, or service).

## Creating Your Manuscript

This is the part of the publishing process that you are always directly responsible for. The quality of your writing depends on your knowledge, skill, and experience. So do your best to learn about good writing techniques for your genre, and learn as much about grammar as you can.

Belonging to a writers' critique group in a related genre with other writers with a similar level of experience to you is very valuable, as is attending writers' conferences and workshops.

By all means ask friends to help you with early editing. But be careful not to depend on them too much. Professional editing is required by many publishers; it is advisable for all authors. And by "professional" I don't just mean that you pay someone who claims to have a gift. Find an editor who has several years of experience and whose previous projects you can sample. Professional editing is one of a few ingredients that make a book the best it can be.

Take ownership of other decisions about your book too. If you plan on including images, what do you want them to look like? What format works best for your book? What ideas do you have for the cover? Back cover copy should clearly tell a potential reader what the book is about and whet their appetite to read more. Make sure you can clearly articulate what the book is about. Make sure that you have an e-book version.

There will be a team of people working on your book. Trust their expertise. Listen to their advice. But remember, it is your book. You are ultimately responsible for content and presentation. If you are not convinced that a particular publisher will do what is needed, keep searching for one that can.

Many writers, editors, and agents have informative blogs that give advice about different aspects of writing and publishing.

# CHOOSING A PUBLISHER

In my experience, the labels used for different types of publisher are not so important as the details of what each publisher is offering. Also, many terms are out of date and the definitions have been conveniently forgotten. The terms can be misleading because some publishers use terms like "traditional model" as a way of boosting their legitimacy because "traditional publishers" usually have the best commercial success with books. Few people want to be labeled with terms like "self-published" because such terms have negative connotations. On the other hand, terms like "royalty" and "wide distribution" are attractive, so publishers like to use them.

As authors we need to closely examine what each publisher is offering (and what they are not offering) and not assume that we know what they mean by the terms they use. Also we need to decide what we really need for our book, and what the fair price is for what they are offering. So be prepared to dig for precise information about what is on offer, and ask good questions. Now, when I say, "ask good questions," I mean ask most of them of yourself—be polite to publishers! But don't be afraid to ask some questions of them.

## The Models

Gardening provides a good illustration of the publishing options that are available to you.

Some people want a well manicured landscape to wow the neighbors, but they prefer to keep their fingernails clean. Perhaps they have more money than time. These people hire a landscape company to design and create the garden of their dreams. They deliver new topsoil, excavate beds, and plant the best nursery stock.

A few people love to be their own experts. They take courses on every aspect of gardening from propagation of plants from cuttings, grafts, and heritage seeds, to the intricacies of aphid life cycles. Perhaps these people have more time than money. They know and love soil. Every spare moment (including the rain-soaked ones) is spent somewhere in the yard.

In between those extremes, people make choices about what they will do themselves and what they prefer to pay someone else to do.

Publishing works like that too. Let's look at three generalized models: Traditional publishers—authors get paid, "self-publishers"—authors pay them, and self-publishers—literally, because the author does the work (I will call this "DIY publishing" for the sake of clarity).

My terms and definitions are deliberately simplified. The two ends of the publishing spectrum (traditional and DIY publishing) are easiest to understand. A multitude of publishers fall between the extremes.

**Traditional Publishers (Royalty, Legacy):**

If you are offered a contract by a true "traditional" publisher it will feel like winning a prize to have your entire yard landscaped by professionals and the photos posted around the world. Your costs will be minimal and potential sales are huge. Here are typical features of traditional publishers.

- Selective about which manuscripts they will accept for publication. The process often begins with a proposal from an author and might even require an agent. Agents get a reputation with editors for spotting good work, so they have special access to the acquisitions editors of some publishers. Agencies and individual agents usually have websites. Guides to publishers may list agents. The "acknowledgements" sections of books usually thank the agent. An interested publisher will ask for a manuscript. You cannot choose to be published this way—the publisher chooses. Having a series of books and a platform of potential readers helps make you more attractive ("Platform" is best explained by Michael Hyatt in his book under that title). A well-know weakness of this arrangement is that it can take months to get a response to an enquiry. Some publishers also take 12-18 months from signing a contract to publication.

- Charge no fees for editing or publishing your book. These publishers invest *their* resources in your book. It is in their interest to make your book succeed.

- Editing is more often in-house. In other words, the publisher controls the editing process and standards. Take some time to read a few titles and judge for yourself their editing standards. Traditional publishers may not give you as much say as you would like in the final content and design of "your" book, but if they know what they are doing, trust them. However, I have been surprised by lax editing in a few long-running best-sellers.

- Ask for the rights to publish your book and sell the rights for translations, movies etc. This frightens some authors. But be clear about what you are really signing away. You are giving the right to print and sell your work as widely as possible in return for a royalty. Traditional publishers often have the greatest potential to sell your book. If your book is truly valuable to readers then giving publishing rights to a publisher that can maximize sales in the widest possible market is the best thing you can do. So long as your book keeps selling, the rights are valuable to you both. If the book doesn't sell, why would you want your rights back anyway? And why would a publisher want to withhold them from you? Rights will only be worth more to an author than to a publisher if the royalties are set wrongly or the publisher is failing to perform. Don't be afraid of signing rights away—but make sure your publisher can do what is needed or that you have an escape clause (return of rights to the author) in the contract in case they fail. Also, be careful that Print on Demand (POD) does not lock you into a contract forever because the book never goes out of print. If you have plans to use parts of your work in other ways then discuss that with the publisher and see if those plans can be allowed for in the contract.

Traditional publishers will register copyright and other official documentation for you.

• Pay authors a royalty and sometimes an advance on royalties. More about this later, but for now note that advances are like loans on future royalties. What happens if your book does not sell enough copies to cover the advance? Will you be required to pay back the balance? Make sure that you understand how your royalty will be calculated for each type of sale (different formats, Amazon, bricks-and-mortar bookstores, and other sales avenues often have different royalty structures). Royalties from traditional publishers are often a smaller percentage than those from other publishing models *but* the potential for higher sales numbers often outweighs the lower royalty per book. The simple formula is:

Profit = (number of books sold × royalty paid per book)

- Author can purchase copies at a discount from the market price. Understand what you will be charged for your books. Are you required to buy a certain number of books? Do you get a bulk discount? What is the likely print cost for your book and how does your purchase price compare to the print cost? Is the publisher's mark-up fair on you?

Since we have begun to talk about the financial side of publishing, it is important to note something right away. Publishing is a business and everyone wants to profit. You as an author would *like* to do well, the publisher *must* do well to stay in business. So don't be unrealistic about costs. Whichever model you choose will involve a significant investment. Most authors do not make any profit; they write because they have other goals. As you consider expenses and potential profits (or royalties), try to be as realistic as you can about what things cost.

- Have access to wide distribution networks for your book. These days most publishers can distribute books widely through the various companies and services offered by Ingram Book Group. But make sure that as many corners of the potential market for your book as possible are covered. Traditional publishers will often have access to specialized markets. The machinery is well-oiled.

- They are also more likely to provide a team of publicists that can promote your book. This is one of two factors (reputation and publicity) that is most likely to set traditional publishers above all the other choices. These days, traditional publishers are attracted by an author's platform because they anticipate sales to that platform. But if you have a good platform, why do you need a traditional publisher? Will the publisher add to what you are already able to do?

- Because of the reputation of this model, traditional publishers are taken most seriously by reviewers, the media, and bookstores. "Traditional" does not necessarily mean that a publisher has been around since the printing press was invented. The term is used of the business model and includes most or all of the above features. The "traditional" model is well respected but don't assume that every publisher that operates under this model is your best option. Even if you like all the details of the above features that a publisher is offering you, what is their reputation as a publisher? Are they known to produce a good book? Do their books in your genre sell well? Publishers with just a few years' experience can still be worth considering if they are committed to excellence and are beginning to gain respect. In every one of these models, a lot rides on the reputation of the publisher. Traditional publishers are most likely to have the best reputation with booksellers, reviewers, media, and readers. However, some publishers using the "traditional" label do not have a reputation to make them worth considering.

Exercise: Over a period of months, compile a list of everything you need to see (or not see) in a contract. Look at sample contracts to get ideas.

What does the contract say? What does the contract NOT say? Make sure that your assumptions are in writing, not just in your mind.

Remember, you are party to the contract so you have a say too.

What is your budget for your book? How long are you prepared to wait for publication?

### "Self-Publishers" (Partners or Hybrids)

This is the jungle category because it includes so many publishers. In essence, this group includes any publisher that falls between the true traditional model and DIY publishing. Some publishers blend a few traditional features into their packages. But the distinctive features are:

- Many charge a fee (sometimes the idea is that the author subsidizes the production—hence the term "subsidy publisher", or shares the expenses—hence "partner publisher" or "co-publisher"). Like the landscaper, you pay them to produce your book. But you can expect to have more say about content and appearance than some traditional publishers will allow. You will need to do more work too. Fees can vary quite widely. Find out exactly what you are getting for your money! When we look more closely at what goes into producing a book and what is on the menu at many self-publishers, we will talk about costs. Make sure that you know what the fair cost is for the main menu items so that you can decide where a publisher's fee fits on the scale.

- Who will own the rights? Just because a company says "you own the copyright" does not mean you own the rights! Copyright protects from plagiarism; rights pertain to publishing and selling the work. If a publisher is happy for the author to keep the rights, is it because they do not expect, or need, to make money from sales of your book? Perhaps they make their money from the fees paid to them by authors like you!

- Less selective. This means that you have a lot more opportunity to go into print and to decide who prints. Some publishers in this category will have a selection process to determine whether your book fits their genres and is up to their standard. Others will take money from vain wanna-be authors and print almost anything (hence the term "Vanity Publisher"). Don't be flattered by acceptance letters that tell you how wonderful your manuscript is; be objective. It is easy for a publisher to claim selectivity, but are they really that selective? One way to tell is to peruse their catalog of titles and genres.

- Offer higher royalties per book. Again, find out how your royalty will be calculated for each type of sale. And remember, the potential number of sales is likely to be lower than a traditional publisher. Some companies boast

100% royalties on certain kinds of sale. It sounds great, but will many books sell through that channel? In the case of these publishers the formula is more like:

Profit = (number of books sold × royalty paid per book) − initial fixed expenses

- Will you be required to purchase a certain number of your own books? If so, how much will you pay (compare the price to printing cost)? This is another way for publishers to make money from authors. The practice is not unreasonable, but make sure the numbers and prices are fair. Most authors will struggle to sell more than a few hundred copies to family, friends, and acquaintances. If you don't have a broader speaking or writing platform, don't get stuck with a garage full of books!

- May sub-contract some parts of editing and production. That is not necessarily a bad arrangement, but make sure the publisher really controls quality and timeliness. Look at several previous publications. If possible, talk to their authors to find out their experience? What do booksellers think of the publisher's end products?

- Distribution and marketing. Nowadays it is easy to claim wide distribution, but do bookstores actually *stock* their books or are they merely *available* in a huge database of books waiting for a customer to order from the store or online? Is the publisher able to sell to libraries (through a distributor called Baker and Taylor)?

- Some publishers in this category have overcome the stigma that attaches to vanity presses and self-publishers; they have gained a reputation for quality books. Again, much of the success of your book will ride on your publisher's reputation. Think carefully about which books and authors you want to be associated with. Even if your book is well written and produced, putting it alongside other books that are known to be poorly done will tar yours with the same brush. Discuss this with a few bookstore managers if you can.

It is easy to sell authors the easiest parts of the production process! Be an informed buyer—not a target for a salesperson.

One warning about "self-publishing companies": If the company makes a significant proportion of their income from the fees they charge to authors then *you* are their potential customer. One clue comes from the number of titles a publisher puts out in a year. The higher the number, the more likely it is that a publisher makes money from the author. And, potentially, manuscripts are being fed into a "sausage making machine" and the books that result are likely to be poorer quality. If a company makes most of their money from book sales then they have more reason to be careful about what they publish and to make an effort marketing books.

So, when you start exploring this kind of company, enjoy interacting with the staff but bear in mind that the company might be most interested in selling *you* a publishing package. Watch out for "limited time" "special" offers on package prices. Marketers know that people like to snatch up a bargain; but the best decisions are made after consideration, not impulsively. Although staff may be good at answering your questions and following up on you, how much interaction will you have *after* signing their contract? Try to discern how excited they really are about publishing your book. If someone says they "loved your manuscript," how much did they actually read? Don't be flattered (it could be like getting your hair caught in the sausage making machine). Stay objective about what is required in order to accomplish your publishing goals.

One way to find out what a publisher is like to work with over the long term is to ask some of their authors about their experience.

Examples of such companies are Xulon Press, Dogear Publishing, and the Author Solutions group of imprints.

A few traditional publishers have started "self-publishing" companies as a way of finding new authors. These companies minimize their investment risk because authors pay a fee. But if a book does well and an author promotes it successfully then the parent publisher has a chance to offer a traditional contract. Examples of such companies are Westbow Press (a division of Thomas Nelson and Zondervan) and Creation House (Strang).

### DIY Publishing

In this model you might be the avid gardener who does everything yourself. More likely, you are a general contractor finding your own sub-contractors. Neither approach is for the faint of heart. They both require huge investments of time and are risky because you have so much to learn about the industry. Many authors choose this model because they have time and think they can save money—they often lose both. Don't forget, unless you have already succeeded at this, you are a novice in a complex business and you will likely learn the most from your mistakes. And, be honest—you have little or no reputation as a writer and publisher.

Some established authors are beginning to DIYpublish. However, they already know how the publishing industry works, they have numerous contacts, and (most important) they have built a platform of fans that are most likely to buy future books. Such authors are attracted by how easy it is to produce books today and by the potential for greater returns on investment from this model. But *you* are not an established author.

Some companies will sell you a package of tools to set up your own publishing company. Before you are lured into a purchase, make sure you know what you can do yourself and what you really need help with. It is easy to sell the easiest parts of the publishing process! Publishing consultants are also available to help for a fee. And you do not have to start your own publishing company; CreateSpace and other sites have very user-friendly websites that make it easy for you to get in print.

- By definition, you will not be selective about your own book. Certainly you will do your best as you write it, but no one is there to be objective about quality and marketability.

- Royalties don't apply. Instead, you will receive all the profits on sales from your book. But again the number of sales will depend on much more than the quality of your book. Can you sell enough copies to cover your initial outlay? Only then will you move into profitability and you might reach the limit of your marketing abilities long before you make a profit. The formula in this model is something like this:

  Profit = [number of books sold × (price per book − expenses per book)] − initial fixed expenses

- Since the author is in control, it is possible to publish a complete book in a very short time if desired.

- Distribution is difficult. In the other two models, publishers pay distribution companies to market and ship books, and to provide a returns service for unsold copies. You will have to pay those fees or do the distribution yourself without offering bookstores the benefit of a returns service. Some basic distribution is provided to many DIY publishers by the printer (e-book and audio distribution is easy). Libraries and other markets are a hard sell.

DIY publishing comes with a stigma because anything can be published and there is little quality control—reputation is minimal where it matters. Many ordinary readers are not averse to author-published books, a few people find such authors appealing. But the stigma within the publishing industry and among bookstores will make it more difficult to achieve broad sales.

To make money in this model, it helps to be a prolific writer. Each title builds your platform and reputation and can gradually increase your profits. Are you able to write prolifically? Can you maintain relationships with fans using social media and newsletters?

Probably the main thing an author gets from this model, aside from freedom of choice, is experience.

Examples of companies that facilitate DIY publishing are: CreateSpace (owned by Amazon), Smashwords, and Lulu.

## The Menus

The following is a list compiled from the websites of several "self-publishers." Not all the items are necessary for every book. Most basic packages include a core list; more extensive packages are offered at higher prices. Some companies will offer *à la carte* services. The rule in all these cases is to know what you really need for your book project and know what the items actually cost. Make sure everything is laid out before signing a contract so that you don't end up having to buy more services that you did not budget for. This list is a representative sample:

- Author education program.

- Author representative to guide you through the process.

- Manuscript critique. (This is not a full edit. The critique is designed to recommend the level of editing that your manuscript needs.)

- 5-20 complimentary copies. (Nice, but what are these actually worth and what are you paying for them?)

- Options on paperback/hardback/audio/e-book formats.

- Discounts on author copies. (How many are you required to buy? Compare the price to printing costs.)

- Author account (for you to track your royalties).

- Royalties. (How are they calculated for different formats and different sales channels?)

- Non-exclusive contract (you keep the rights to your book).

- Editing (up to 50,000 words)—Decide for yourself who will do this best, but make sure a professional is involved at some point. There are different types of editing available: developmental, copy edit, proofreading. Developmental editing comes first and requires an extensive knowledge of the author's idea for the book, and familiarity with the manuscript. A developmental editor will suggest the best sequence or storyline for the book, chapter themes, and perhaps titles. Copy editing focuses on grammar and punctuation (spelling should be quite clean by this stage). Proofreading is a detailed check for mistakes.

Not everyone needs a developmental editor, but every author should have a professional editor thoroughly check the manuscript. Poor editing will ruin an otherwise excellent book. What will you pay for extra editing if your manuscript is more than the number of words included in the package? What do other levels of editing cost?

- Back cover copy writing—needs to include keywords that will help readers find your book on a website. What word or phrase makes the best search term for finding your book? My book about the names of God needed to have "names of God" as a keyword phrase in any online description and in the sub-title (I chose not to use it in the title because that title is used in several other books and is rather bland).

- Category—Amazon and other online booksellers have categories for books to help readers find them. Make sure your book is in the appropriate categories (3-5 category entries depending on the bookseller).

- Indexing service (creating an index in non-fiction and reference books).

- Design, layout—the book has to be formatted in a pleasing and consistent way. It must also be done according to very precise specifica-tions given by the printer. This part of the production process is quite technical and least likely to be tackled successfully by an author. Printing companies frequently require manuscripts to be submitted in a format that requires specialized software (Adobe Indesign). However, there are plenty of people in the industry who can do this well. If a publisher can't excel at design or layout (and at a reasonable price) RUN.

- Cover design—Attractive covers do help to sell books. Again there are plenty of skilled cover designers out there. Shop around for prices and quality.

  Don't rely on a good cover. Once a book is on a shelf with the spine facing out, people won't see the cover. Some publishers can pay some booksellers to arrange titles "Face Out" on the shelf for a while. But you need to make sure people hear about your book in other ways. Choosing a good title and listing it in the correct category are essential, as we shall see later.

- 10-50 image insertions.

- Printing—another menu item that can be done well by many printers. Again, if a publisher does not excel at this at a reasonable price, RUN. We shall see later that one high quality printer dominates the industry in America, but local printers might be an option in some cases.

- Distribution and a returns service—for most authors, these things are essential, and easy for a publisher to provide. Most books are printed and flow seamlessly into a distribution network. If booksellers cannot sell a book, they are able to return it to the distributor. Publishers pay a relatively small fee for the returns service, though it might be proportionately more for smaller publishers.

No publisher can guarantee that bookstores will carry a book, so don't be misled. Bookstores are separate entities and make their own decisions about which books they stock based on knowledge of their customers and the profit they need to make on a book.

Exercise: Be brutally honest with yourself about how broad your readership can be. Is it limited to family and friends, focused on a local interest, professional group, or society? Is the quality of your writing good enough to give your book wide and long-lasting appeal? What is the shelf-life of your book (depends on the subject matter)? For instance, a book about the 2012 Olympic Games quickly loses interest.

Based on the answers to those questions, do you REALLY NEED national or international distribution (beyond Amazon and the internet)? If you are not actively marketing to a national market, you do not need national distribution (because few people will know about your book anyway).

- Publicity and marketing—these days, most publishers expect most authors to drive publicity. If a publisher offers some aspect of this in a package, ask yourself how much it is really worth. Are they offering frills or valuable tools? A tool that results in measurable sales has measurable value. So ask around to find out which sales tools really work? What value do author promotional videos have? Are you really likely to use that 4000-address mailing list? And what would it cost to mail all those postcards anyway? (10-15 cents per postcard plus 39 cents per stamp.) If the publisher offers you a website or a web page, will people actually find it? Will the publisher use the best keywords (see below) for your book?

Should you hire a publicist? That is a hard question to answer because the least expensive publicists are likely to do the basic things that you might be able to do yourself. The more a publicist charges, the more likely it is that they have valuable contacts and a reputation that gets the media's attention. Good publicists are expensive. Whether you hire one will depend on your budget. But be very careful of what a publicist really can do; your best gauge is their track record. Few publicists will guarantee results, or work on commission.

- Catalog advertizing (but do booksellers pay attention to the publisher's catalogs?).

- Tradeshow representation (better if you can attend to represent your own book).

- Registration with national online booksellers and distributors (this should be standard).

- Registration with Books in Print database (this should be standard).

- ISBN, LCCN, Copyright registration, EAN Barcode.

- Marketing tools including press releases, printed materials, book signing kits, website, shopping cart, social media campaigns, and e-mail marketing.

- Video trailer.

- Keywords and categories (Amazon)—the biggest marketplace for books is the internet. The biggest bookseller on the internet is Amazon. The problem is that almost every book in print is listed there and it is hard to make your book visible. Just as it is hard to see the cover of books arranged on a bookshelf, so it is hard to find your book on the internet unless it is correctly "cataloged".

The internet is like a humongous library of information. Amazon is an online store with a section dedicated to books. Your book must be listed in the category (or categories) that accurately reflect its subject and content. Keywords are another way of highlighting the subject matter of a book so that readers are more likely to find yours if they are searching in that subject. Keyword and category selection are very important and sometimes require extra knowledge to do them well.

A note on Amazon search results: With millions of books in print, some categories and subjects have thousands of books to choose from. If your book is not in the top page or two of search results, it might as well be on a dusty bookshelf in a dark corner of a dying bookstore. In order to make your book more visible to potential buyers you need to understand as much as you can about how Amazon decides which books to put first in the search results. No one knows exactly how because the algorithms are secret, but it has to do with sales, price, availability, and keywords. In the absence of the secret formula, do your best to maximize each of them. You may have opportunity to experiment.

As you consider which publishing model to use, remember that the end goal for your book includes sales. You want your book in the hands of a certain type of reader. An important question to ask is whether the prospective publisher actually sells books in the right marketplace, the place where your desired readers look for books. What is their track record like? How many books on similar subjects or in the same genre do they publish and sell?

Even if your publisher does little or nothing when it comes to promoting your book, will they support *your* efforts at marketing and publicity? Make sure that you will not be let down. Are they going to add something valuable to your own marketing efforts?

If a publisher provides valuable (i.e. effective) publicity for your book and can accomplish all the other menu items effectively, take that publisher very seriously. Publicity is essential for book sales to go beyond what the author can accomplish.

Exercise: Look at the packages offered by different publishers (Xulon Press, Westbow Press, CreateSpace, Dogear Publishing, for example) but research your own prices for items too. Learn to ask good questions about the pieces in the packages.

## The Math

### Offset vs POD

Print on Demand (POD) is the ability to print a book soon after it is ordered. The process is made possible by the internet and sophisticated electronic presses. An order placed on the Amazon website will often result in a warm book in a mailer box within hours. The biggest advantage is that no one has to store a pile of books. The disadvantage is that POD availability can be taken as a sign of a publisher's expectation of minimal sales. Offset publishing is done to fulfill orders of more than 1000 books. Savings per book are huge but someone has to store them. Publishers choose this option when they are confident of sales.

Lightning Source is the largest printer of books in the USA. They are able to do POD and offset printing. Their service interfaces very efficiently with publishers and with the main distributor, Ingram Publisher Services. Ingram Group owns both companies (and several others in the industry). IPS provides software to bookstores that includes their catalog of all the books they print (ipage). Booksellers can easily look up books and place orders. Regional warehouses help speed the distribution of books that are printed offset and kept in stock. Most authors do not have the option of dealing direct with Lightning Source and IPS. Ingram and Lightning Source are not the only way to go, but they are largest and most used.

## RRP

Recommended Retail Price (RRP) is the price printed on the back cover of a book. Booksellers are not *required* to sell at this price; rather it is the price from which their discount is calculated. For instance, booksellers might order a book with a RRP of $24.99 from IPS for 45-55% off that price (about $11.25 - 13.75). The discount a store qualifies for depends on the volume of business that they do.

RRP is decided by the publisher but calculated to allow for set printing costs plus a cost per page. Inclusion of images, quality of paper etc will add to the price. But the RRP is designed to give everyone involved in the process sufficient profit over expenses. Inevitably, as more "middlemen" are involved, the price increases. Distributors need to make money from book sales to bookstores, and publishers will pay a fee for the returns service. Make sure that the RRP and the price a bookstore can buy it for are realistic— that the bookstore can still price it so customers will buy it and the store will make a worthwhile profit. Bookstores will not order books that they do not believe their customers can afford, or that they cannot profit from.

The middlemen include:

- Printer, publisher, distributor, and bookseller.

- In some cases an agent and publicist need a cut too.

## Royalties

Your royalties are usually a percentage of sale price minus expenses. Find out exactly how they are calculated for each publisher and each sales channel and format (e-books often get a higher royalty, Amazon royalties might be different from other booksellers).

## Contract obligations

- How many books are you required to buy for how much and over what period?

- Under what circumstances does the contract terminate?

Exercises: Explore LightningSource.com, Find out about Ingram Book Group.

Ask bookstore owners (that sell your genre of books) which catalogs they look at, how prices work, and how shelving decisions are made. (You could ask them a lot more too!)

While investigating a publisher, find out whether they will give you offset prices if you order more than 1000 copies of your book.

### The Methods (of selling books)

- Online sales, Amazon etc.—65% of e-book sales (Apple and Barnes and Noble are the bulk of the rest).

- 31% of e-book sales are DIY published authors.

- Bricks-and-mortar (Independent stores)—still a significant percentage of sales.

- Libraries—less significant but valuable for books that suit a library (especially reference and non-fiction).

- Author sales—can be a very significant percentage of sales, but it takes work.

Authors typically sell books through a personal website, book signings, book festivals, and speaking engagements. Depending on your subject and gifting, speaking engagements and websites have the potential for the highest author sales.

# ESSENTIALS FOR PUBLISHING

This section is a summary of the main points covered above with a few additions. For a book to succeed in the marketplace the following are not the only requirements but are the most essential.

- Endorsements: Make sure your endorsers are people with as much authority and influence in the field as possible. Endorsers who are only known by a small circle of people are nice but they do little for an author's credibility.

- Professional editing and production.

- Distribution (to the market for your book).

- E-book discounts: A popular strategy to get attention to books on Amazon is to aim for the best-seller list in your book's category. Offering a limited time discount (or free e-book) and publicizing it on social media is simple and relatively inexpensive. A 2-3 day offer can dramatically increase downloads of a Kindle book and result in short term recognition on best-seller lists. That in turn grabs attention. Remember, there is almost no cost for e-books and the royalties are often higher percentages than print books, so you can make money even on a very low priced book.

- Reviews: You as the author have to drive this. Ask prospective reviewers if they would be willing to read your book and write a review in exchange for a free copy of your book. Your investment in this is some time spent researching who reviews books in your genre, the cost of a book, and shipping. Consider this an investment. If you are required to buy a large number of copies of your book it is possible that you will be left with quite a few copies in years to come when you decide to stop your marketing efforts. I comfort myself with the thought that I am disposing of any left over copies ahead of time in the hope that more reviews will result in increased sales. Better to sell more copies than expected and have to order more, than to have them left over when they could have been used as a sales tool.

Goodreads.com is a great place to offer your book to interested readers who might then write a review. Many bloggers review books. There are plenty of websites and Facebook pages devoted to reviews. Reviews can be posted on Amazon, Goodreads, and other online booksellers like Barnes and Noble.

- Publicity: Books never succeed without publicity of some kind. If a publisher is offering publicity and marketing that has proven value (they sell books), then take any offer from that publisher very seriously. This is the most essential piece.

- A realistic RRP, especially if you are interested in sales through bookstores.

www.ingramcontent.com/pod-product-compliance
Lightning Source LLC
Chambersburg PA
CBHW022132280326
41933CB00007B/660